Original title:
The Poet and the Primrose

Copyright © 2025 Creative Arts Management OÜ
All rights reserved.

Author: William Hawthorne
ISBN HARDBACK: 978-1-80566-706-3
ISBN PAPERBACK: 978-1-80566-991-3

Reflections in a Dewdrop

In a dewdrop, a tiny world spins,
A worm in a tux, where the laughter begins.
It slips and it slides on a grass blade wide,
With thoughts of a dance that it can't quite abide.

A squirrel watches, giggles, and grins,
As ants in a line wear their tiny chins.
They march on in rhythm, so proud of their plight,
While whispers of pollen tease in the light.

The Dancer in the Meadow

In the meadow she twirls, with petals a-flare,
A butterfly joins her, as light as the air.
With a kick and a spin, off they dash and zoom,
While daisies dissolve in the sweet spring bloom.

The grass rolls its eyes at their fanciful moves,
And a nearby cow moos, feeling left in grooves.
Yet together they laugh, all the creatures unite,
For fun never stops when the sun's shining bright.

A Sonnet for the Wildflower

Oh tiny wildflower, with your petals so bright,
You tease the tall grasses, much to their fright.
They stand up all proper, with a snobby stance,
While you laugh in the breeze, sparking tender romance.

A beetle rolls by, in a giddy parade,
Exclaiming that beauty is meant for a trade.
But you know that the best blooms with laughter and cheer,
And spread all around, like a sweet song we hear.

Echoes of Nature's Palette

The wind sings a tune, swirls colors anew,
A fox with a brush paints the skies a soft blue.
With laughter and humor, the clouds start to play,
As squirrels draw the outlines, in their clever way.

Amidst the ruckus, a flower peeks through,
Curious about all this colorful hue.
It giggles as colors dance with delight,
While nature's grand party plays on through the night.

The Thread of Nature's Narrative

In gardens where the daisies play,
A quill once danced in bright array.
It scribbled dreams in shades of green,
While worms critiqued the lines unseen.

A butterfly, with wings so wide,
Told tales of love the bees deride.
With every flap, a giggle flew,
In sunny fields, the laughter grew.

The sunbeam peeked, with cheeky grin,
Unraveled knots of leaves within.
The ants staged plays in grand parade,
While shadows whispered, jokes they made.

And thus the world, in jest, unfolds,
With nature's yarn in colors bold.
Each petal burps, each blade of grass,
A stage where whimsy comes to pass.

Blossoms Beneath the Written Sky

Once under clouds, a flower fretted,
For bees had flown, but vainly sweated.
It cheered them up with jokes so bright,
As petals twirled in sheer delight.

A pencil bug with nice round specs,
Took dainty notes on past insect wrecks.
He scribbled fast in laughter's sound,
While nature's giggles swirled around.

A raindrop slipped, a slippery fool,
It splashed on leaves, just breaking rule.
Laughter spread across the green,
As puddles formed a froggy scene.

And underneath that written sky,
Each blossom sang and winked an eye.
With silly prances, nature spun,
In cheeky verse, the day was won.

Nectar of the Written Word

In a garden of whimsy, a quill takes flight,
With a bottle of ink, it's a wild, silly sight.
Words spill like nectar from blossoms so bright,
Bees buzz in laughter, perched high on a kite.

A rhyme tumbled down, tripped over a bee,
Spilled honeyed lines on a bumblebee spree.
Oh, what a banquet, sweet lines for the free,
Bring on the giggles, there's nectar for me!

Palette of the Gentle Sky

A bluebird dabbles in colors so bold,
Painting jokes on the canvas, as stories unfold.
Orange laughs with purple, the humor is gold,
Chasing the clouds, where mischief takes hold.

With brushes of laughter, the sunset will gleam,
The sky winks in rhyme; it's a whimsical dream.
A splash here and there, in this playful theme,
Even stars giggle, it's a light-hearted beam!

Mornings Wrapped in Petal Poesy

Morning wakes up in a blanket of dew,
Whispering tales of the night's funny crew.
Petals are giggling, oh, what a view,
As the sun yawns and stretches, can you believe it's true?

Bumblebees chatter, their dance is a tease,
With pollen on their noses, they twirl with ease.
Petals in pajamas, they sway in the breeze,
Waking the sleepy buds, sharing good cheer, if you please!

Symphony of Dew-Kissed Stanzas

A symphony starts with a sprinkle of mist,
Notes of the flowers, twirling, can't resist.
Stanzas bloom forth with a giggle and twist,
Ever so lightly, in laughter, they exist.

Caterpillars chuckle, they sway on the strings,
Chirping their saltines, oh, what joy it brings!
With melodies sweet, evoking the flings,
In this dew-kissed garden, everyone sings!

Scribes of the Wandering Breeze

A dandelion danced on the wind,
It scribbled notes, how absurd, my friend!
With every twist, it whispered a tale,
Of grasshoppers jumping, quite out of scale.

The bushes giggled, a rustle in the air,
Scribing a song with nary a care.
While worms debated their nightly plots,
And ladybugs giggled in garden spots.

Seasons of Ink and Essence

The maples dripped with ink so bright,
As squirrels scribbled tales of their flight.
The daisies in ruffles, such silly gowns,
Told secrets of sunshine in faraway towns.

The roses, in laughter, began to compete,
With petals adorned like a quirky sheet.
The gusty wind left us all in a spin,
As bees buzzed the chorus, let chaos begin!

Poetic Prowess in Blooming Fields

Oh, forsythias flaunted their sunny flair,
While snippets of phrases flew through the air.
A bumblebee's buzz stole the show,
As purple violets chimed in, woe to toe!

With daisies placing their bets on the breeze,
They cheered on the butterflies, quite at ease.
But the tulips just sighed with a haughty air,
Saying, 'We're blooming, do you even care?'

The Silent Chorus of Flora

In the garden, a silence, though not quite still,
As flowers held court on a soft, gentle hill.
Their giggles erupted, oh, what a play,
As roots tangled, dreaming of what they'd say.

With petals as microphones, they took a stand,
Reciting their verses, a bountiful band.
The sunflowers rolled with laughter so grand,
While daisies debated who'd make the best stand.

Lullabies in Leafy Embrace

In a garden where giggles bloom,
The daisies all wear a hat of gloom.
Butterflies dance with silly flair,
While grasshoppers sing without a care.

A frog croaks out a comic tune,
As crickets tap beneath the moon.
The roses roll their eyes and sigh,
'Why does that frog always act so spry?'

A Glimpse Through the Green

Peeking through leaves with a wink and grin,
A squirrel bumbles, can't help but spin.
The sunbeams chuckle, bouncing bright,
As flowers join in—what a silly sight!

Jasmines whisper jokes to the bees,
While ferns unfold like giggling seas.
A daffodil mocks a passing leaf,
'You think you're slick, but I'm the chief!'

Harmonious Firmament and Flora

Underneath the cosmic jest,
Stars chuckle at nature's best.
Dandelions dance with pride and glee,
Swaying along with a bumblebee.

Violets tease the sun's warm light,
'You think you're hot? We're pretty tight!'
Laughter echoes through the vale,
As blooms unite—what a joyful tale!

Whispers from a Flowered Heart

Bees buzz tales, both small and grand,
As petunias tap their tiny hands.
Lilies giggle, tucked in their beds,
While daisies spin like tops on heads.

Tulips claim a crown of cheer,
Their petals swaying, loud and clear.
Nature's stage is set for fun,
Where every laughing flower has run!

Musing in the Flowery Haven

In a garden where daisies grin,
The bees argue who'll take the spin.
Butterflies dance and giggle with glee,
While ants march on with grand jubilee.

Petunias whisper scandalous tales,
Of secret meetings behind the pails.
A ladybug dons its finest attire,
As sunlight glimmers like sparkling fire.

Tales Born in Blossoming Gardens

A rose once claimed it was the best,
But tulips laughed, 'You need a rest!'
Daffodils snickered in bright yellow hats,
While sunflowers nodded, looking quite fat.

Each flower a character in this spree,
Vying for laughter and wild jubilee.
Petals prancing, what a delight,
A garden where humor takes flight.

Enigmas of the Hidden Bloom

There's a mystery behind the fern,
A riddle in petals, oh so stern.
Where do the shy violets hide their grace?
Only dandelions hold the secret place.

A quirky lily think it's on a quest,
To find who's the funniest of the rest.
Winking grasshoppers with all their style,
Crack jokes that make even weeds smile.

Echoing Heartbeats of Greenery

Amongst the greens, a giggle erupts,
As ferns play tag, they twist and cup.
A squirrel pops in for a light snack,
While a crow squawks loudly, 'What's the flack?'

Trees swap stories with rustling leaves,
Of cheeky bugs and muddy thieves.
Laughter ripples through each little nook,
In this merry, botanical storybook.

Symphonies of the Nature's Lyric

In the garden where daisies dance,
A tulip tried to steal a glance.
With leaves that waved in mock salute,
It tripped on roots, oh what a hoot!

A bumblebee sang quite off-key,
While ladybugs laughed with glee.
They played a tune of buzzing cheer,
As ants held tiny cups of beer.

The wind chimed in with a gentle blow,
Telling tales of the soil below.
A caterpillar rolled in the grass,
Declaring he'd prefer a nice martini glass!

But under the sun, what a sight!
Silly flowers in broad daylight.
With petals fluffed, they spun around,
In a symphony of joy profound.

The Secret Diary of Wildflowers

In a notebook made of leafy greens,
Wildflowers penned their funny scenes.
An iris giggled with its mate,
"You think you're tall? Oh, isn't that fate!"

A rogue dandelion made a bet,
To grow as high as the sun, you can bet!
Yet every time it stretched so wide,
It got blown away in the breezy ride!

"You bloom too early," a sunflower said,
As it poked fun at the poppy's head.
"You really need to take a rest,
Or else you'll be the flowered jest!"

But when twilight brings its shade,
They tell jokes 'til the next parade.
Oh, secret laughs within the fields,
To funny truths, their charm yields.

Ballad of the Wistful Meadow

In the meadow where the laughter flows,
A clumsy rabbit tripped on its toes.
The flowers giggled, waving their heads,
"Watch out for stumps, or you'll end in beds!"

A butterfly flitted with flair so grand,
Chasing away the clouds that planned.
But with a flurry it hit a breeze,
Fell right down, landing on some peas!

Each bloom held a secret, under the sun,
Of silly fables and good-natured fun.
With petals bright and stories to tell,
They intertwined like a magical spell.

As grasshoppers croaked their nightly tunes,
The fireflies danced like lilting balloons.
In the wistful meadow's warm embrace,
The humor of nature found its place.

Harmonies of Petal and Pen

With ink that flows like morning dew,
The petals sang and the daisies knew.
They scribbled notes, oh what a scene,
As violets dreamed of lavender sheen!

A lilac proclaimed its fragrant charm,
While cacti plotted, "Let's cause alarm!"
They jest about the roses' thorns,
Saying, "At least we don't wear scorns!"

And in the twilight, when shadows play,
The flowers gather for a charade, hey!
The pens take flight, with laughter galore,
As they write their tales forevermore.

In harmonies of petal and pen,
The bloom of joy repeats again.
What a quirky cast, in nature's sketch,
A floral comedy, without a hitch!

Troubadour of the Sprouting Earth

In the soil, a dancer prances,
Singing tunes to sunlit glances.
Worms wiggle in a grand ballet,
While daisies cheer, 'Hip-hip-hooray!'

With clogs made from old tin cans,
He twirls beneath the luckiest plants.
Crickets play a joyful beat,
As beetles stomp with tiny feet.

A broomstick horse, his noble steed,
Together they fulfill the need.
To spread delight on patches green,
In silliness, the world is seen.

Cantata of the Springtime Waltz

The morning dew begins to hop,
As tulips sway and giggle non-stop.
A dance of petals, wild and free,
With bumblebees in harmony.

The robin's got a hat that's tall,
He trips, he flutters, then takes a fall.
He shakes it off with a cocky flair,
Soon enough, he's soaring through air.

A chorus of frogs by the pond's edge,
Crooning love songs, they make a pledge.
To serenade the blooms all day,
In a froggy, frolicking ballet.

Garden Sylphs and Scribbled Lines

In a plot where gnomes take naps,
Sylphs spin verses with funny chaps.
They write on petals with glittery pens,
While ants chip in with their tiny friends.

One writes about a quirky worm,
Who thinks he's a prince, with lots of charm.
He bows to daisies, takes a leap,
And dreams that lilies sing him to sleep.

They giggle as they paint the air,
With script that dances everywhere.
Oh, the tales this garden spins,
Where nature laughs and joy begins.

Fragrance of Unwritten Lines

The scent of laughter fills the air,
As flowers plot a grand affair.
Dandelions toss their crowns in glee,
Painting wishes as far as the eye can see.

Breezes whisper cheeky thoughts,
While shadows play with clever knots.
Each petal writes its cheeky tale,
In fragrant ink, they never fail.

A breeze kisses the playful blooms,
As butterflies dance to their tunes.
In this patch of whimsy land,
There's humor tucked in every strand.

Silhouettes of Echoing Whispers

In shadows dance, a tale unfolds,
Where whispers laugh, and secrets hold.
A figure sways with a crooked grin,
While petals giggle, as they spin.

Beneath the moon, a prankster plays,
Sipping nectar in moonlit haze.
A chorus sings, in silly cheer,
As flowers tease, then disappear.

With every twist, a chuckle shared,
A symphony of mischief declared.
The breeze tells tales of silly sprouts,
In the garden of giggles and shouts.

So if you spy, a dancing bloom,
Join in the fun, forget the gloom.
For every snooze, a bloom awaits,
In pockets of laughter, fate creates.

Petals and Phrases Alight

A flower spoke in rhymes so sweet,
With petals soft, and dancing feet.
It tickled bees, with jokes anew,
While butterflies burst out in "Boo!"

Through morning dew, shenanigans rise,
As daisies wink and pull surprise.
With every breeze, and every jest,
The blooms conspire, they jest and jest.

In sunny spots, they play charades,
While squirrels munch on flower blades.
"Did you hear?" the violets tease,
"A rose fell down, oh wouldn't that please!"

So gather 'round, let laughter bloom,
In gardens rich, dispelling gloom.
For every flower with a quirk,
Can turn a day to a joyful perk.

Ink Drop on Leafy Canvas

Upon a leaf, an ink drop falls,
It spills a tale, that giggles calls.
Each mark a chuckle, each splotch a grin,
As stories swirl, we dive right in.

A squirrel grins, a feather writes,
As crickets chirp through sunlit nights.
The ink runs wild, with splashes bright,
While shadows dance, with sheer delight.

A canvas made of nature's art,
With every stroke, it plays the part.
It mixes laughs with drops of rain,
A recipe for silly gain.

So grab your pen, and let it flow,
In leafy worlds where giggles grow.
For laughter blooms in every line,
An ink drop's dance is truly fine.

Tracing Sunlight with Stanzas

In sunlight's gaze, the stanzas jive,
With silly lines, they laugh and thrive.
They twist and turn, with playful grace,
As bright rays tease each flower's face.

The daffodils shout, "A rhyme to hear!"
As sunbeams bounce, and cheer them near.
With every line, a joke unfurls,
In the theater of floral swirls.

A laughter spills, from roots to sky,
As bumblebees dance, and buzz nearby.
With every turn of playful phrase,
The garden spins, in sunny haze.

So pen your verses, let joy ignite,
In sun-drenched fields, where hearts feel light.
For tracing beams with jolly jest,
Will bloom a world that's truly blessed.

Gossamer Threads of Thought

In a garden full of laughs,
A flower wore a silly hat.
It danced with all the butterflies,
Saying, "Can you top that?"

With petals bright and cheeky grins,
It tickled every breeze that blew.
The sunbeam chuckled from above,
"What mischief next for you?"

A ladybug joined in the fun,
Trying to waltz, but missed the beat.
"I'll spin you right round!" it declared,
And tumbled off its tiny feet.

The flowers giggled, grass did sway,
In this hilarious floral spot.
Each thought a thread, a woven play,
In a world where giggles never stop.

Strokes of Nature's Brush

A painter came with colors bold,
To brighten up the garden scene.
He spilled some yellows, blues, and golds,
And tripped on something green.

He painted daisies, made them dance,
Then found a rose that won't stand still.
"I swear this flower has a prance!"
His palette slipped, oh what a spill!

The petals laughed, as paint flew high,
A canvas of chaotic fun.
The butterfly exclaimed, "Oh my!"
"Art's best when you can run!"

The artist chuckled, washed in hues,
His fingers turning shades of glee.
In nature's studio, bright with muse,
Every dip brought pure esprit.

Inked Impressions on Velvet Petals

In a lovely patch, the ink ran wild,
An artist tried to sketch a bee.
But all he drew was a laughing child,
Sipping nectar with such glee.

The petals whispered silly tales,
Of flowers wearing funny shoes.
The ink smeared out like fishy gales,
As daisies giggled with their hues.

A bumblebee buzzed in and said,
"Your art is grand, but where's the fun?"
So they created a floral spread,
With polka dots for everyone!

The colors blushed, the petals bright,
In a playful, whimsical spree.
The garden danced with pure delight,
As ink and laughter wild and free.

The Muse Within the Meadow

In fields where laughter blooms and grows,
A muse emerged with a twinkling eye.
It tickled flowers under their nose,
And made the wind burst out with a sigh.

The daisies danced like they were mad,
While clouds above chuckled in delight.
The butterflies fluttered, feeling glad,
As the sun began to giggle bright.

Each blade of grass swayed in a sway,
Joining in the cheerful parade.
The muse whispered, "Come out to play!"
And nature's giggles, never fade.

So if you wander through this cheer,
With flowers beaming, you might find,
A world of whimsy waits so near,
Where laughter blooms and hearts unwind.

Verses Carved in Green

In a field of chatter, blooms so bright,
The flowers debate in morning light.
One claims to be the fairest of all,
While bees just buzz and have a ball.

A squirrel rolls by, with antics to share,
Declaring himself the best gardener there.
He digs up the roots, no reason in mind,
While petals giggle, oh how unrefined!

The daisies wink, the tulips snicker,
Tiny ants march in their dance, much quicker.
Each stem a storyteller, tales to expose,
Of a garden gossip that only they know.

So in this patch where laughter blooms,
Nature's comedy dispels all glooms.
In green verses written, a frolic to see,
In the realm of plants, there's always glee!

A Tapestry of Glades and Stanzas

Amidst the leaves, the laughter rings,
Where daisies host a band of kings.
The thorns argue who's sharper and bold,
While marigolds trade stories of gold.

A rabbit writes with clumsy paws,
Drafting epics of adventuring draws.
The mushrooms chuckle at his plight,
Holding a contest for the silliest plight.

Frog poets croak their slippery lines,
Riffing on tales between the pines.
Each line is a leap, each verse a jump,
Creating a frothy, fun-loving thump.

So in glades where stanzas twirl and sway,
Nature's humor steals the day.
Crafting tales from petals and grass,
In a tapestry of laughter, none let it pass!

Melodies Beneath the Blossom

Under petals where the mischief plays,
Mice write symphonies in furry ways.
With tiny flutes and acorn drums,
Bouncing to rhythms, the band hums.

Birds compose, with chirps so bright,
Tales of the cat that danced at night.
While butterflies twirl in a funny ballet,
Critiquing each note, in their own whimsical way.

Honeybees buzz their buzzing beats,
While ants march in for rhythm retreats.
Creating a concert, a wild display,
Nature's melodies leading the day.

So beneath blooms, where laughter clings,
A world of buzzing and fluttering sings.
In this symphony of chirp and cheer,
Every note a chuckle, loud and clear!

The Language of Colorful Days

Upon dandelions, wisecracks flow,
Colors engage in a vibrant show.
The blues claim they know all the laughs,
While reds burst forth, crafting math in halves.

Orange tells jokes, notorious for guffaws,
While lavender sighs, updating its cause.
The greens roll their eyes at silly riff,
While even the whites get in on the jiff.

With splashes of hues, the garden's in tune,
As the clouds drift by humming a tune.
Each petal a phrase, each leaf a pun,
The canvas of days, a colorful run.

So languages blossom, each hue a jest,
In a riot of tones where laughter's the quest.
From morning to dusk, they dance and sway,
Turning ordinary hours into funny ballet!

The Chronicle of the Sun-Kissed Garden

In a garden where laughter grows,
A sunflower tells the tale of woes.
The carrots dance in their orange suits,
While gossiping beats play on trumpets of fruits.

A tomato slipped on a daffodil's dress,
The bees just buzz, causing no stress.
With daisies giggling, the day takes flight,
Their petals shine in the warm sunlight.

The chubby gnome rolls in the grass,
He swears he once raced a cunning sass.
While daisies wink at the cheeky thyme,
Who whispers jokes without a rhyme.

So join the party where blooms unite,
In a sun-kissed garden, oh what a sight!
With each petal's chuckle, we find delight,
And leave our troubles hidden from the light.

A Tapestry of Life's Fragile Beauty

In a meadow where stories twine,
A butterfly sips on sweetened wine.
With every flutter, a giggle is spun,
As daisies parade in the warm sun.

A ladybug tickles the leaves with glee,
While tulips argue who's tallest, you see.
The breeze carries whispers from flower to flower,
In this delicate realm where laughter's the power.

Oh, the violets jest with jesters in bloom,
Creating a chorus that brightens the gloom.
While the shadows play tag with the sunbeams bright,
Here lives a world bursting with mirth and light.

So gather your chuckles, your giggles, your cheer,
In this tapestry woven with love and with beer.
For life's fragile beauty won't last all day,
But while it's here, let's laugh and play!

Songs Linger Among the Grass

In the greens where the crickets croon,
A frog in a crown thinks he'll be a boon.
With a hop and a splash, he joins in the fun,
While ants march around under the setting sun.

The grass is a stage for bubbles to float,
A ladybug belts out her high-pitched note.
While dandelions sway like they're on a spree,
They're teaching the daisies how to be free.

The wind plays a tune though it's just a breeze,
As petals tap dance in tune with the trees.
And jokes travel far on the wings of the bee,
In this symphony sweet where all are carefree.

So come make a rhyme, let your worries be cast,
In the grass where the laughter is always a blast.
For every song sung, and each blustering laugh,
Is a testament bright to our joyful path.

Paintings in the Morning Light

As dawn spills colors across the sky,
The flowers wake up with a stretch and a sigh.
A rose puts on lipstick, a daffodil's hat,
While marigolds giggle at the antics of cat.

In the early hours, they hold a grand show,
Where petals paint pictures in a vibrant glow.
A tulip gives warnings, 'Don't step on my toe!'
While pansies play poker with seeds in a row.

As shadows recede, they dance with delight,
Twisting and twirling in morning's soft light.
With laughter and cheer spilling over the land,
These paintings of joy surely were planned.

So let's grab a brush and join in their game,
Crafting our moments, nothing is the same.
In this colorful world where smiles take flight,
Forever our hearts dance in morning light.

Whispers of Yellow Blossoms

In a patch of sunshine bright,
A flower giggles with delight.
It sways and twirls, a funny dance,
Chasing ants with reckless prance.

A bee zips by, it's quite the sight,
The bloom gives chase, oh, what a flight!
'Catch me if you can!' it seems to say,
But stout little bee gets lost today.

With laughter soft, the petals tease,
While squirrels play tag with utmost ease.
The grass stands tall; it can't sit still,
For nature's laugh can't fit the bill.

So here we sit, these blossoms bright,
Wishing more days were filled with light.
For in this dance, there's joy and cheer,
A funny world we hold so dear.

Verses Amongst Petals

Petals fall like jelly beans,
In a garden full of scenes.
A squirrel wears one on his head,
A fashion trend that's widely spread!

The breeze whispers silly rhymes,
As nature's clock just skips the times.
A dandelion sings a tune,
While bees join in; it's quite the swoon.

Blossoms giggle in the sun,
While cheeky bugs prepare for fun.
A ladybug dons shades of red,
Claiming it's the garden's spread!

Let's toast to flowers, wild and free,
Who dance and sway with glee and glee.
In this valley of laughter loud,
We bloom and laugh, so very proud.

Serenade of Spring's Gentle Bloom

A tulip sings, 'Come look at me!'
While posing just beneath a tree.
Its petals stretch, a grand display,
As if to shout, 'It's my birthday!'

The daffodils join in the tune,
Bowing low to the sun and moon.
A chorus of colors, bright and bold,
In the flower bed, their stories told.

And here come clouds with hats askew,
But sunshine plays a peeking deer.
With a soft wink and playful tease,
The blooms erupt, oh what a breeze!

So laugh along with petals fair,
In this garden where joys declare.
A serenade of spring's own beat,
With colors dancing, oh, so sweet.

Ode to the Delicate Sunlight

Oh sunlight creeps in, oh what a sight,
Kissing flowers, making them bright.
A lazy bee rolls in delight,
Singing, 'I'll nap here, this feels right!'

Daffodils dip for a chat with the grass,
As a breeze swirls, it's quite the class.
A butterfly slips into a warm hug,
While daisies wink at a passing bug.

A flower shimmies in the soft light,
Calling friends to join the invite.
A lilting laugh, a song unheard,
And all the petals dance, absurd!

So here's to warmth and laughter, dear,
In gardens where there's naught to fear.
With every bloom and every ray,
Let's play along and joke away!

The Dreamer among Moonlit Blossoms

In a garden lush and bright,
A dreamer twirls with sheer delight.
He trips on petals, slips, and falls,
While laughing at his dopey calls.

The flowers giggle, swaying low,
As he wobbles, putting on a show.
With every step, a new surprise,
A bumblebee, a startled sigh.

The moonlight dances on his face,
His silly moves, a perfect grace.
He spins with joy, a comical breeze,
Who knew dreams came with such a tease?

With every bloom, a grin is cast,
In this moonlit world, he's unsurpassed.
He chats with daisies, what a sight,
In this silly realm, everything's right.

A Journey Through Sunlit Fields

In fields of gold, where shadows play,
A traveler stops to jest and sway.
He greets a squirrel, who looks bemused,
While chasing after nuts, quite confused.

Butterflies join, a fluttering dance,
He spins around, caught in a trance.
"Hey there, friend! Care for a race?"
The squirrel darts off, gives him a chase.

The wildflowers lean in for a peek,
At his antics — oh, the joy they seek!
He tumbles down, a dusty roll,
The sunflower laughs, a spirited soul.

The sun shines bright, a silly crown,
As he frolics through this leafy town.
With every step, he leaves a smile,
In sunlit fields, he's lost for a while.

Whispers of Blooming Verse

Among the blooms, a secret chat,
A daisies' club with a jolly hat.
They whisper tales of summer fun,
While weaving rhymes 'til the day is done.

A lilac chimes in, all aglow,
"Have you seen that bee? He's quite the show!"
They giggle and nod, as petals croon,
In the breezy air, under the moon.

The daisies bloom with stories old,
Of silly ducks and gardens bold.
In this flowered row, the laughter swells,
With petals dancing, laughter glows and dwells.

What fun it is to share in verse,
With colors bright, there's no need to rehearse.
As shadows stretch, they sigh with glee,
In this living poem, wild and free.

Starlit Sonnet in the Garden

Beneath a sky where twinkling lights,
The garden hums with wondrous sights.
A clumsy cat pursues a mouse,
Right through the blooms, oh what a rouse!

The stars above, they giggle bright,
At the hopping feet in the pale twilight.
"Do flow'rs can dance?" they whisper in awe,
As blooms bounce back to nature's law.

The roses chuckle, petals wide,
As the cat takes another wild slide.
With every pounce and every spin,
He ends up tangled in vines — oh, what a win!

A sonnet born from laughter's grace,
In this garden, a wiggly race.
The moon beams down with a wink so bold,
As nature's whimsy, forever told.

Garden of Rhythms Untold

In a patch of bright green, a flower sits,
Winking and grinning, throwing bits.
"Why talk with a bee when you can hum?"
It twirled in the breeze, oh what a fun drum!

With roots that tickled the worms below,
They laughed as they danced, putting on a show.
A squirrel rolled by with a nut in tow,
Shouting, "This garden's a real flower show!"

The carrots joined in, all dressed in orange,
They sang with delight, no need to estrange.
"If you plant a joke, will the laughs grow tall?"
A riddle in petals—let's share them all!

In this wild place, where giggles abound,
Plants sport their jokes, swirling round and round.
With dirt on their leaves and smiles in each vein,
The fun never ends in this gardening game!

Painting with Words and Blooms

With petals like paint, on a canvas so bright,
A sunflower stretched, reaching for height.
"If only I had legs, I'd do a dance!"
It wobbled with glee, nearly lost its chance!

The daisies chimed in with giggles and cheer,
"Dance like our blooms, no need for a peer!"
A bee took a spin, wearing its fine coat,
"I buzz with delight, let's all take a note!"

Every blade of grass buzzed with a grin,
Swaying like dancers, letting joy in.
"A tickle from raindrops, a splash in the sun,"
In this garden of laughter, there's always more fun!

With colors like laughter that paint the air,
Each bloom shares a joke, with not a care.
The canvas of nature, forever in bloom,
With whimsy and fun, it brightens the room!

A Harvest of Natural Verses

In fields of green, where the crows like to party,
A tomato stood up, declared it quite hearty.
"I'm ripe with good humor, just like my skin!"
With seeds of laughter, let the day begin!

The pumpkins convened, all round and all bright,
"We may not be smooth, but we laugh with delight!"
They shared silly stories that twisted and twirled,
As vines intertwined, they danced and they whirled!

"Carrot top jokes are the best of the bunch,"
Said one leafy green, munching a lunch.
"Why did the cabbage refuse to play fair?"
"Because it couldn't find a partner to share!"

So harvest these moments in soil and in sun,
Where nature is silly and life's full of fun.
A patchwork of laughter, where verses are sown,
In the garden of giggles, you're never alone!

Enchanted Grove of Starlit Lines

In a grove alive with twinkling starlight,
A gnarled old tree told tales through the night.
"Did you hear the one 'bout the moon's silly grin?"
It chuckled so hard, it nearly fell in!

The owls hooted back, wearing glasses so round,
"We study the stars, but laughter is found."
They dressed up the night with a shimmery glow,
While crickets composed a whimsical show!

With branches like arms, they waved hello,
To each passing breeze, in the soft flow.
"Why do the stars avoid poker at night?"
"They can't handle the bluff—it's a cosmic fright!"

So gather your giggles beneath twinkling skies,
Where stories and laughter take flight and arise.
In this enchanted realm, light-hearted and free,
Every shadow whispers, come dance with me!

Where Petals Hold Secrets

In the garden, whispers bloom,
Petals giggle, banish gloom.
Bees are jesters, buzzing loud,
Wearing pollen like a shroud.

Daisies tease with sunny cheer,
Sowing laughter, drawing near.
Roses wink, their thorns all fake,
Joking softly, 'It's no mistake!'

A Dance with Spring's Quill

The breeze brings tales from afar,
Written by a twinkling star.
Frogs compose their silly tunes,
While daffodils don party balloons.

Worms recite with wiggly flair,
In grass skirts, with style to spare.
A rabbit hops, joins the beat,
With all the critters, oh so sweet!

Nature's Ink on Paper Soft

With petals dipped in sunlight's rays,
Nature scribbles silly plays.
Ants march proud, their lines so neat,
In leaf scripts, they pen their feat.

Clouds take quizzes on their heights,
While snails compete in silly flights.
Mice write tales on grassy pages,
Boundless laughter through the ages.

Serenade of Garden Dreams

A sunflower steals the show tonight,
Winking at the moon's soft light.
Fireflies blink with secret codes,
As daisies dance in little toads.

In the orchestra of buzzing bees,
Nature's humor brings us ease.
Petals sway, they tell a joke,
A garden's laugh, a gentle poke.

A Bloom Among Shadows

In a garden where whispers blend,
Lurks a flower who thinks she's a trend.
She giggles at bees with a smirk,
Claiming nectar's her quirky perk.

As the sun casts its playful tease,
The bloom dons her petals, aiming to please.
But her friends, oh, they roll their eyes,
Saying, "It's just dirt and the blue skies!"

A shadow doth creep, seeking her fame,
She laughs, "I'm too cute to be part of this game!"
In silence, the weeds just shake their heads,
While the flower prances, dreaming of threads.

Yet in the end, as the twilight glows,
She yawns and admits, "Just a garden, I suppose!"
Her petals all crumpled, but her spirit's still bright,
Embracing the shadows, she sings through the night.

Secrets in Soft Petals

Beneath a leaf, a secret lies,
A blossom swears it hides from prying eyes.
"What do you hide?" asks a curious breeze,
"A dance of the daisies, if you please!"

In whispers, they chuckle, tossing their tales,
About how the sunbeam sometimes fails.
A dainty petal with an attitude grand,
Claims she can dance better than the band!

But wait! here comes a squirrel, oh dear,
His antics too funny, his laughter sincere.
The flower laughs and rolls her eyes,
"Keep it down, or I'll bloom with surprise!"

Yet deep in the dusk, when the moon takes flight,
They share their secrets, the laughter, the light.
In soft petals, under stars so wide,
They find joy in the wonders that they cannot hide.

Ode to the Gentle Blossom

Oh gentle bloom, so shy in the field,
You curl up tight, yet your charm's revealed.
With petals so soft, like whispers of spring,
You sway with the breeze, what joy you bring!

But wait! A butterfly, perched for a chat,
Says, "Promise to let me come back for a snack!"
With grace, you nod, and roll your sweet eyes,
Knowing full well how quickly time flies.

Yet when the rain falls, and the jellybeans drop,
You wobble and giggle, and can't help but bop.
Those puddles are mirrors, a show just for you,
Reflecting the fun in each raindrop so new!

So here's to you, in your squishy attire,
Life's silly moments, you never tire.
A bloom on this stage, forever you'll chase,
The laughter and joy that you sweetly embrace.

The Lure of Sunlit Meadows

In meadows sun-kissed, where daisies dance,
Sunshine's a tease, a bright, bubbly chance.
A flower named Giggles, wears petals of gold,
Sings tales of bees, both silly and bold.

"Catch me if you can!" she calls with a twirl,
As a playful wind gives her a whirl.
The grass roars with laughter, joining the fun,
While clouds in the sky whisper, "Oh, what a run!"

A ladybug hears and joins in the spree,
They laugh as they weave through the grand old tree.
"You think you're so clever with colors so bright!"
Giggles just grins, her spirit takes flight.

With each sunny moment, her joy multiplies,
In the lure of the meadow beneath wide blue skies.
And as day turns to dusk, she hums her sweet glee,
For tomorrow awaits with more games and decree!

Ink-Stained Petals

In a garden where ink spills bright,
Flowers giggle at the sight.
A daisy dons a scribbled hat,
While a rose waves at a chatting cat.

The violets tease, they've got no shame,
Their tales of dirt put some to blame.
A splash of color on every pail,
With each blush, a cheeky tale.

Bees buzz by, in fits of laughter,
Wondering 'bout what comes after.
A pot of paint spills on the ground,
Now every petal wears a frown.

Yet when the sun dips low and bright,
They dance along with all their might.
To the humor of nature, whimsically free,
Painted petals, their jesting spree.

The Garden's Secret Melody

In the quiet of the leafy dance,
Frogs croak jokes as if by chance.
A fern tells puns in swaying grace,
While rabbits chuckle in their place.

A toad serenades with a croaky tune,
While bees are buzzing under the moon.
The lilies sway, not missing a beat,
Their harmony's truly a funny treat.

In corners where shadows play and tease,
Squirrels join in with a chuckling breeze.
For here, the flowers are jesters bold,
Their laughter a story, forever told.

So if you wander to this lively realm,
Take a seat on nature's helm.
And listen close, hear the giggles soar,
In the melody of the garden's core.

A Blossom's Dreaming Heart

A blossom dreams of being a star,
Wishing for petals shaped like a car.
With wheels of daisies, it zooms around,
Chasing bees that buzz and bounce off the ground.

It thinks of sprouting wings to fly,
Imagining clouds as it slips by.
But oh, the troubles of such a quest,
Tripping on roots, poorly dressed!

In daydreams, it swings from tree to tree,
Hosting tea parties with bumblebees.
But when it wakes, it finds with a start,
Its petals are bare, not a paintbrush of art.

Yet laughter echoes in its heart,
As it learns there's joy in its own part.
For the sunshine blooms tales of pure delight,
In the flower's dreams, it shines so bright.

The Language of Blooming Corners

In secret corners where flowers chat,
A sunflower's tall, calling 'Look at that!'
While tulips blush in shades of glee,
Their whispers float on warm, sweet tea.

Each petal practicing absurd rhymes,
Reciting silly poems, expressing good times.
Through playful pranks and gentle sights,
They hold their meetings on starry nights.

The daisies giggle, their secrets they share,
Of butterflies caught in a net of hair.
It seems that each bloom has a funny story,
In the garden's laughter, there's endless glory.

So wander near these laughing blooms,
Where humor dances and the heart resumes.
For in each petal lies a punchline sweet,
A merry language that can't be beat.

Palette of Nature's Lullaby

In the garden, colors dance,
Chasing bees that skip and prance.
A brush of leaves, a wink of light,
Nature whispers, 'Isn't this right?'

With each petal, a tale unfolds,
Of silly winds and laughter bold.
Dandelions strut in golden glee,
While ladybugs taunt the bumblebee.

A splash of hues, a twist of fate,
The flower's jam is worth the wait.
They giggle as they bloom and sway,
In this colorful game they play.

So grab your shades, let's paint a scene,
Where nature's laughter reigns supreme.
A canvas bright, where jokes take flight,
In this vibrant world, everything's right.

Where Words Meet Wildflowers

A wildflower's chat, so bright and spry,
Engages clouds that drift on by.
They gossip 'bout the earth below,
As butterflies play tag, you know?

Each bloom a word, so fresh and bold,
Weaving stories that never get old.
The sun joins in with a cheeky grin,
While ants march by, their tiny kin.

"Who wrote this chatter?" the daisies plead,
"The wind, I swear, took just the lead!"
They laugh so hard, petals shake and sway,
As bees buzz secrets, hip-hip-hooray!

In this meadow, joy's on display,
Where words meet wild blooms every day.
With every breeze, a joke takes flight,
A tapestry of laughter, pure delight.

Serenade of Sun-Drenched Blooms

Sun-kissed petals sing a tune,
To the lazy sun, oh what a boon!
Grass tickles toes while squirrels skit,
As flowers groove, they can't help but split.

A rose and lily, best of pals,
Swap tales of mischief, oh the gales!
The tulips sway with a cheeky laugh,
While bees join in, doing their math.

"Who needs a stage?" the daisies jest,
"We've got the ground, we're truly blessed!"
With every petal that flutters and spins,
They're the stars of this sunny scene of wins.

So let's dance wildly, under the sun,
With each bloom bursting, laughter's begun.
In this floral concert, we find our way,
A serenade of joy, come laugh and play!

Petal-Scented Reverie

In a meadow, dreams take flight,
With scents of petals, what a delight!
Thistles and thorns join in the fun,
While daisies twirl, their day's just begun.

A buttercup sings, "I'm quite the star!"
While violets debate the best candy bar.
With whispers of breeze, they jest and tease,
As nature giggles, doing as it please.

Chasing shadows, hiding from each other,
A bouquet of laughter, my flowery brother.
The sun winks down, feels quite jovial,
A painting of petals, all so colorful!

In this fragrant realm, all's merry and bright,
With each blooming joke, we dance into the night.
A petal-scented world, let's frolic and sway,
With laughter and blooms, we'll play all day!

Ink and Floral Dreams

In a garden of scribbles, blooms take flight,
Each petal a word that dances in light.
The ink spills laughter, a whimsical spree,
While flowers throw parties, wild and free.

A daffodil winks with a cheeky grin,
As pens join the party, let the fun begin!
The tulips gossip in bright yellow suits,
While daisies wear hats made of curly roots.

The rose rolls its eyes, 'What a silly scene!'
With quills like party hats, oh what a green!
The sun, like a DJ, spins bright tunes,
Gathering joy from the laughing blooms.

So here's to the fun in the garden's glow,
With ink on our hands, we steal the show.
In floral fantasies, let the laughter gleam,
For every good story starts with a dream!

Echoes in the Morning Dew

In the early light, where whispers play,
The flowers argue who's bright and gay.
Twirling around in a morning haze,
They share their secrets in delicate ways.

A bumblebee buzzes, demanding attention,
"I'm the star here, with every intention!"
But roses just snicker, their petals held high,
"Please, you're just here to sip and fly."

The lilacs chuckle, with voices that mingle,
"We're the real art, they're just here to tingle!"
With droplets of dew like gems on the grass,
Each bloom gets a moment, no need to surpass.

So let's raise a toast to the morning cheer,
Where each floral buddy is lovingly near.
With echoes of laughter, and petals that sway,
Together in sunshine, we'll brighten the day!

Chasing Daybreak's Fragrance

As dawn tiptoes in, a curious sight,
The blooms wake up with sheer delight.
"Who's stealing the sun?" a sunflower shouts,
While morning glories giggle, in kind beouts.

A daisy declares, "It's my time to shine!"
With petals spread wide, feeling simply divine.
But lilies respond, "Just wait for a while,
You'll see who stands tall with the biggest smile."

Petunias dive in, with colors that sing,
While sprigs of thyme jest about the ring.
With every soft sigh, and laugh that ensues,
Chasing the fragrance, in playful hues.

So let's tip our hats to the day that's begun,
With humor and mischief, we bask in the fun.
In a patch of wild laughter, where dreams often blend,
We're a bouquet of joy, with no need to pretend!

Rhapsody of Earth and Ink

With colors so vivid, the canvas sprawls wide,
Each bloom is a line, on nature's wild ride.
A bud claims its space, with a sassy flair,
While petals hum tunes in the sweet, warm air.

The marigolds chuckle, "We shine like the sun!"
With ribbons of orange, they sow seeds of fun.
In the garden of giggles, where laughter's a tune,
The ink spills like rain, let's dance with the moon.

The phlox throws a bash, "Bring your best joke!"
While wise old trees nod, as if they're bespoke.
Each line in the soil breathes joy and glee,
With whispers of stories, forever carefree.

So here we create, with a splash and a wink,
In a rhapsody wild, with both earth and ink.
Together we flourish, in quips that we weave,
For life's but a garden, where we love to believe!

Chronicles of the Sunlit Path

In a garden where sunlight plays,
A little flower giggles and sways.
It winks at bees with a cheeky grin,
As they dance around, drawn from within.

A squirrel pauses, tilts its head,
Hoping for crumbs, or maybe some bread.
The flower just chuckles, looking quite spry,
'You'll have to earn it! Now don't be shy!'

The sunlight beams with golden cheer,
As butterflies flutter, spreading good cheer.
Each petal a joke, each leaf a rhyme,
Nature's humor, so simple, so prime.

And when shadows lengthen, the laughter won't cease,
For in this garden, joy finds its peace.
The stories of sunlight, so light-hearted say,
That fun is the best at the end of the day!

The Muse Beneath the Softest Leaves

Beneath the shade where whispers roam,
A ticklish breeze finds a cozy home.
A ladybug giggles, all spotty and bright,
Chasing its dreams in a flicker of light.

A snail rolls its eyes, so slow and refined,
'You'll never catch me! I'm far too aligned.'
The ladybug sighs, 'Let's pick up the pace,
You'll miss all the fun in this loveliest place!'

As petals gossip, exchanging old tales,
About dewdrops, raindrops, and whimsical trails.
Nature's soft laughter, a gentle parade,
Reveals our odd quirks in the games that we played.

When dusk drapes the sky in hues of delight,
The whispers continue, just out of sight.
The stars twinkle boldly, joining the glee,
For even the night loves a light-hearted spree.

Captured in the Arms of Green

In a meadow so lush, where mischief blooms,
A rabbit with sass hops and zooms.
It mocks the old hedgehog, grumpy and shy,
'Catch me if you can, don't just stand by!'

The hedgehog grumbles, 'I've got my own flair,
With my quills, my friend, I'm the one you should scare!'
But the rabbit just chuckles, a comic delight,
'There's no need for quills when you can leap high!'

The daisies are laughing, bending with mirth,
As sunlight spills joy all over the earth.
Each blade gives a giggle, a tickle, a tease,
In this playful world, nature aims to please.

As twilight approaches, the air hums with fun,
With fireflies glowing, their dance just begun.
A celebration of life, where laughter arrays,
Captured in green, in the longest sunrays.

The Heart's Offering to the Earth

Once upon a time, in a whimsical nook,
A flower made wishes, with a skip and a look.
It sent out its hopes in a sweet little breeze,
Drawing in laughter from the wise old trees.

'Oh, give me a friend!' the flower did plea,
'One with a zing and a laugh just like me!'
But the trees chuckled softly, roots deeply grounded,
'Life is the punchline, and fun is unbounded!'

As clouds drifted by with a sprinkle of cheer,
The flower kept dancing, devoid of all fear.
With raindrops applauding, the sun joined the song,
'Together we'll flourish, where everyone belongs!'

The earth cracked a smile, embracing the day,
For laughter is magic in its gleeful way.
An offering of joy to the sky and the soil,
In this heartful exchange, all hearts would uncoil.

Harmonies of Leafy Whispers

In a garden where giggles grow,
A leaf lost a dance, oh what a show!
The flowers leaned in, they laughed so bright,
As bugs waltzed on by, what a sight!

With petals that tickle the summer breeze,
They play hide and seek with rustling trees.
A squirrel in a hat, looking quite dapper,
Screaming at clouds, 'You better not caper!'

A daisy slipped, oh what a flop,
While bees hummed away, daring non-stop.
The sun winked down, with a cheerful gleam,
Join in, dear friend, it's all quite a dream!

So come take a stroll through this jolly patch,
Where giggles and harmony all seem to hatch.
Among leafy whispers, let laughter creep,
And dance with the blooms, let merriment leap!

Sketches Under the Shade

Under leaves where shadows play,
Lies a chubby bug, lost in the day.
With a top hat made from an acorn cap,
He taps his foot, taking a nap!

Nearby a twig takes a fancy curve,
While butterflies glide, ready to swerve.
What's that a tomato exclaimed with glee,
'I've finally grown, look at me!'

A lizard, in shades, sunbathing so fine,
Comments on styles, 'I've started a line!'
The ants roll their eyes, busy as ever,
While the clouds look down, playing faux tether.

Sketches of life, in colors so bright,
Nature gathers, preparing for night.
With laughter and mirth, they all relate,
Under the shade, isn't it great?

Echoes of Blossoms Past

In a meadow where giggles echo loud,
A daffodil danced, proud of her crowd.
With petals that shimmered in morning gleam,
She twirled in circles, living the dream!

A tulip called out, 'Please steal that show!'
While bees sported shades, in a polite row.
The daisies chimed in, their heads held so high,
'We're blooming with laughter, just watch us fly!'

A spider spun tales from an aged web,
As vines twined around, ready to ebb.
But wait, did a rose just sneeze with flair?
'Allergies strike!' was her loud, lovely scare.

So echo the blooms as they giggle and sigh,
In a frolicsome world under the sky.
With whispers of joy spreading far like the past,
Let laughter ring out, as shadows are cast!

Unfolding Stories in Silken Hues

In the garden of tales, where colors unfold,
A butterfly flutters, wearing a coat of gold.
With stories to tell, she spins in delight,
Of a snail who raced under the moonlight.

A poppy piped up, 'I'll join in the fun!'
While petals got tangled, all bright like the sun.
'Oh look at us go, what a fancy parade!'
Said a lily, who bloomed, proud of her braid.

The grass chuckled softly, pretending to sleep,
While ants held a conference, secrets to keep.
A worm grinned wide, with laughter and cheer,
'In this tangled tale, we're all pioneers!'

Unfolding their stories, in silken hues bright,
A whimsical world danced in pure light.
With every snapshot, a giggle would rise,
In the garden of tales, where laughter flies!

Reverie Where Wild Things Sing

In a garden where oddities play,
Laughter twirls in the sunlight's ray.
A squirrel recites on a tiptoed limb,
While daisies nod, and the daisies swim.

A flamingo practiced a silly jig,
Wiggling around like a drunken pig.
The bees, they buzzed, a comical choir,
As grasshoppers leaped and jumped higher.

Butterflies wearing outrageous hats,
Gossip about the gophers and rats.
Each bloom has tales that they like to spill,
In whispers so sweet, on the edge of a thrill.

When the sun dips low, shadows collide,
As nature's jesters perform with pride.
With every petal's giggle and grace,
Springtime's laughter fills every space.

The Elixir of Flowering Words

Words sprout like daisies after rain,
At the tip of my pen—oh, what a gain!
Roses gossip with violets on the side,
While tulips burst forth, with nothing to hide.

As a rhyming bee drifts by with a grin,
Sipping sweet nectar—where do I begin?
Each verse, a sip from the chalice of cheer,
Awash in petals, I'm buzzing—I'm here!

Puns dance around in the lily pad mist,
Where humor's the blossom no one can resist.
Charming sunlight dresses all words in gold,
Filling each cup with stories retold.

In this garden of laughter, come take a look,
Each verse is a petal, a page from a book.
With whimsical blooms that tickle the mind,
In flowers' embrace, the best thoughts unwind.

The Soft Dance of Nature's Ink

With ink made of sunshine and laughter,
Nature scribbles with joy and with rapture.
A bumblebee draws circles in the air,
While petals pirouette without a care.

The willows sway like they know a secret,
Rumors of rocks that giggle and creak it.
Even the clouds play peek-a-boo high,
While crickets tap dance, oh my, oh my!

A lark takes a bow, a solo complete,
As daisies clap with their dainty feet.
The breeze whispers jokes to the sleepy pines,
And tulips blush as the humor entwines.

In this comic ballet, all nature concedes,
Joy blooms in places where no one proceeds.
With giggles and grins, around every bend,
Nature's soft dance is the world's best friend.

Rivulets of Thought in Petal Streams

Thoughts flow like streams through the meadow's embrace,
In ripples of laughter, they quicken their pace.
Each petal a note in a merry refrain,
Dancing with whimsy, I can't help but gain.

Wiggly worms tell tales that twist and curl,
Where daisies declare, "Oh, what a swirl!"
Buttercups chime in with giggles galore,
As thoughts tumble forth from the green pasture floor.

The cloud's shape-shifting, a jester in the sky,
While marigolds wink and the sun waves goodbye.
Laughter bubbles up from a brook's cheeky grin,
As petals float by in a whimsical spin.

In this stream of musings, one truth holds clear,
Each flower and thought whispers, "Let's cheer!"
Together they weave a delightful bouquet,
Where humor and nature unite in the fray.

www.ingramcontent.com/pod-product-compliance
Lightning Source LLC
Chambersburg PA
CBHW072116070526
44585CB00016B/1473